D1164266

Santas

WOODCARVING
· with Rick Bütz ·
STEP BY STEP

Santas

Rick and Ellen Bütz

STACKPOLE
BOOKS

Published by
STACKPOLE BOOKS
5067 Ritter Road
Mechanicsburg, PA 17055

Printed in the United States of America

10 9 8 7 6 5 4 3 2

First edition

Cover design by Tracy Patterson

We have tried to make this book as accurate and correct as possible. Plans, illustrations, photographs, and text have been carefully researched. However, because of the variability of all local conditions, materials, personal skills, and so on, Stackpole Books and the authors assume no responsibility for any injuries suffered or damages or other losses incurred that result from material presented herein. Carefully study all instructions and plans before beginning any project.

Library of Congress Cataloging-in-Publication Data

Bütz, Richard
        Santas / Rick and Ellen Bütz. — 1st ed.
            p.   cm. — (Woodcarving step by step with Rick Bütz)
        ISBN 0-8117-2566-9
        1. Wood-carving. 2. Wood-carved figurines. 3. Santa Claus in art. I. Bütz, Ellen, 1950-   . II. Title.
    III. Series.
    TT199.7.B886   1995
    731.4'62—dc20   95-3763
                                                                                                                CIP

To Dad,
who introduced me
to the enjoyment of woodcarving

Contents

Working on these Santa figures will help you master a variety of carving techniques. I think you will enjoy each project.

Getting Started

There are few projects that I enjoy more than Santas Claus figures. With their bright colors and cheery faces, they are a joy to create. And, they make wonderful gifts.

If you have ever wanted to learn face carving, Santas are a great place to start. In this book I will show you two different techniques for carving faces in complete, step-by-step detail. Once you master these techniques, you can enjoy making all sorts of figures with a wide variety of expressions. All it takes is sharp tools and a little practice.

The projects in this book are arranged from simple to more complex. So, if you choose to work your way through the book from beginning to end, you will receive a complete course of instruction in Santa carving techniques.

However, if you prefer, jump right in and start with whichever project appeals to you most. Each project is designed to stand on its own; all the information you need to complete it is provided. You will also find full-size patterns and complete painting instructions with each project.

If you find you have questions about a particular step of the carving, just refer to the section of the book where that technique was first introduced for some additional hints.

WOOD

Around the world carvers use hundreds of different varieties of wood. In my classes I encourage students to try carving any piece of wood they can get their hands on. Many little-known or local woods can produce excellent carvings.

However, for small carvings like these Santa figures, I have two particular favorites: air-dried white pine and basswood. Both have a fine, even grain and smooth texture that hold detail well. Also, both woods are light colored, which makes them ideal for painting.

Finding wood can be a problem for beginning carvers. I haunt the local sawmills and buy a year's worth when I find some I like, but you may want to start with smaller quantities. For most of my projects I try to get boards about 2 inches thick.

Often the wood is green, so I dry it myself for a few months before I begin carving. To dry green wood, I store it in the loft of my garage, or under my workbench. I always put some small strips of wood underneath the boards to lift them off the floor, and between the individual boards in a stack. This allows for good air circulation and ensures even drying.

Your best source of supply will usually be

other carvers. Try joining a local club. In every group of carvers there is someone who knows someone who has a great supply of wood and will be happy to sell you a few pieces.

In addition, most of the mail-order companies that sell carving tools also sell small blocks of carving wood. See the Resources section for a list of suppliers.

LIGHTING

You don't need a lot of space or equipment to enjoy woodcarving. All you need to start are a comfortable place to sit and a sturdy table. Natural light is best to carve by, but incandescent lights will work well too. Avoid fluorescent light, which is too soft and diffuse and does not cast enough shadows to show clearly the shapes when you are carving.

TOOLS

The most basic and versatile carving tool is a good knife. I prefer one with a comfortable wooden handle and a short, straight blade. The blade should be about 1½ inches long, made of good carbon steel. You may also find that a few carving gouges will be helpful.

Throughout this book I will list the gouges that I used for each project. These are only suggestions; you don't need to purchase every tool I mention. Use what you already have on hand and feel free to substitute one tool for another of similar size and shape. With a little experimentation you will discover the tools that work best for

you and begin developing your own personalized tool kit.

Whatever tools you choose, they have to be razor sharp. Sharp tools are a joy to work with. They slice off precise chips and leave a smooth, polished surface. Dull tools will crush and tear the wood, making your carvings look crude and splintery no matter how carefully you make the cuts.

Sharpening is such an important subject that I have devoted an entire book in this series just to sharpening. Refer to it for tips on how to maintain a perfect cutting edge on your tools.

Experienced woodcarvers know that a sharp tool is safer than a dull one: it requires less force to move through the wood, and it is less apt to slip and cause injuries.

However, sharp tools must be treated with respect. So before you begin, take a few minutes to study the following carving methods. Practice on a piece of scrap wood until the techniques begin to feel natural and you have an understanding of how to use your tools safely. This will save you a lot of frustration in the long run.

CARVING

There are two safe ways to carve with a knife. The first is called the paring cut because the basic motion is like peeling a potato. Brace your thumb on the carving and slowly close your hand as you draw the knife through the wood. Position your thumb on the carving so the knife will not touch it as it cuts through the wood.

The paring cut

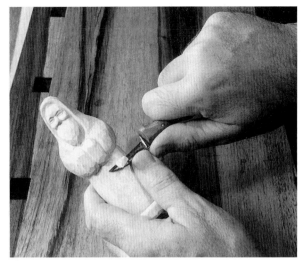

The levering cut

The second cut, called the levering cut, is handy for reaching places that are hard to carve with the paring cut. Brace the thumb of your left hand against the back of the knife blade and pivot the knife using your left thumb as a fulcrum.

These two methods give you the best control for removing wood safely. With these two techniques and a sharp knife, you can carve all the projects in this book. If you are left-handed, just reverse the hand positions.

For safety, relax and take your time. Don't try to remove big chunks of wood with a single cut. There is an old woodcarver's saying that's worth remembering: "Three small chips are better than one big one."

Above all, never hold the wood in one hand and pull the knife toward you with the full force of your arm. This is dangerous because you have no control over the knife. Woodcarving is a process of removing small chips of wood with control and precision. When carving, always keep the fingers of both hands braced on the wood for the greatest control and safety.

You can also use woodcarving gouges on these projects, especially for shaping fine details. To do this, the same safety rules apply. Keep the fingers of the hand holding the tool braced on the wood. Never push the tool through the wood with the full force of your arm while holding it with your other hand. If the tool slips out of the wood with

The pencil grip for carving fine details with a small gouge.

that much uncontrolled force behind it, the results can be disastrous.

The first technique for using a gouge safely is called the pencil grip. Hold the blade of the tool just like a pencil, between your thumb and index finger. Use these two fingers to gently push the blade through the wood in a series of short cuts while the rest of your fingers are braced against the wood. For even more control you can rest the shaft of the blade against your middle finger. Notice that the fingers of the hand holding the carving are out of the path of the tool for added safety.

A more advanced technique for using gouges safely is one I learned from the master carvers of

The Swiss technique is an alternate way to carve with a gouge. Grip the wood and tool as shown (left) and carve with a sliding motion (right). Always keep the thumb of the hand holding the tool braced on the wood for safety and control.

Brienz, Switzerland. This technique will be used for carving the final project in this book, the Swiss St. Niklaus.

Hold the handle of the gouge in your closed right hand and brace the outstretched thumb of your right hand against the wood. To guide the tool, slide the shaft of the blade along your thumb as you move the tool with a slight motion of your wrist. Resist the temptation to push the tool through the wood with the force of your arm. Always have your thumb braced on the wood for safety and control.

This technique may feel awkward at first, but the fine control it gives makes it well worth mastering.

In a sense, woodcarving is different from any other art form because as a woodcarver you must learn to work in cooperation with your material. Woodcarving really develops a sense of learning to "go with the flow."

Wood is made up of bundles of microscopic, hollow fibers called the grain. These tubelike fibers carry nutrients and moisture up and down the trunk of a tree. They also determine the direction you can carve when you are working with a piece of wood.

If you are carving and notice your tool is raising splinters and making a rough, crunching sound, even if it is sharp, then you are carving against the grain. Woodcarvers try to avoid this as much as possible.

Whenever you find yourself carving against the grain, simply carve from the opposite direction. When you carve with the grain, your tool will pro-

Carving against the grain

Carving with the grain

duce nice, clean shavings and leave a polished surface on the wood.

Carving with the grain is mostly a matter of developing a feel for it. It's a bit like petting a dog or cat. One way feels right and the other way doesn't. And, like your dog or cat, the wood will quickly let you know which way is right.

As a final note, when your carvings are done, always sign and date them. After all, you have created something special and a bit unusual. With care, woodcarvings will last nearly forever and be passed down for generations. Years from now people will enjoy knowing who made the carvings they now treasure.

Alpine St. Nicholas

Our image of Santa Claus as a plump, jolly, old man dressed in red is actually an American custom dating back only a hundred years. It began with the drawings of Thomas Nast, which appeared in *Harper's Weekly* from 1863 until 1886. These in turn were inspired by the poem "The Night Before Christmas," by Dr. Clement Moore.

However, the tradition of St. Nicholas dates back nearly a dozen centuries to a certain early bishop of Myra in Asia Minor. His reputation for generosity and acts of kindness, especially to children, became legendary.

In remembrance, the Feast Day of Nicholas in December has always been celebrated by giving gifts to small children in the saint's name.

Over the centuries, the image of St. Nicholas became part of the folk culture of many European countries and often varied from one region to the next.

This particular woodcarving is a style that has been handed down through my family for several generations. It is a German folk carving technique developed high in the Bavarian Mountains. In these isolated Alpine villages the woodcarvers often worked with only a few simple tools—usually a sharp knife and perhaps a carving gouge or two for fine details.

The wood they used was the native pine that grew abundantly in the mountains, giving rise to the name Black Forest.

During the winter, small figures like this St. Nicholas were often carved as gifts. These figures traditionally had a somber or even stern expression, unlike the jolly, smiling Santa we know. They were clothed in traveler's cloaks of blue, green, or brown, with thick fur collars to keep St. Nicholas warm.

I really enjoy carving these figures, especially when snow begins to fall here in the mountains. As the fragrant pine shavings curl away from my knife, it is easy to imagine a woodcarver from long ago. I can picture him sitting snug and warm in his mountain cottage as the wind and snow swirled around shuttered windows. Light from a crackling fireplace revealed the shapes of the woodcarving, as chip by chip a tiny St. Nicholas appeared from the block of wood, as if by magic.

Today, it's still like magic to me. Each woodcarving I make seems to have a unique personality of its own. No two are ever just alike.

I think you will enjoy carving these figures as much as I do.

ALPINE ST. NICHOLAS

Tools

Carving knife
Detail knife
3mm no. 12 V-gouge
Paintbrushes

Materials

Air-dried white pine or basswood
    5 1/2 inches by 2 1/2 inches by 2
      inches
Acrylic paint
    titanium white
Oil or alkyd paint
    phthalo green
    burnt umber
    burnt sienna
    cadmium red medium
Enamel paint
    gold

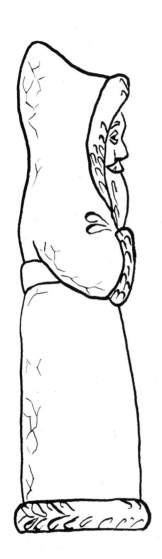
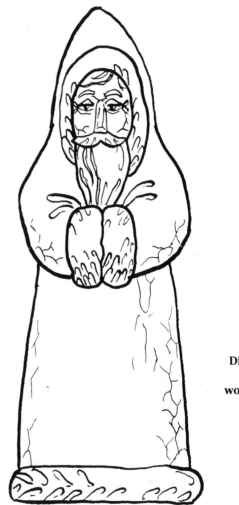

**Direction
of
wood grain**

Begin with a piece of air-dried white pine or basswood at least 5 ½ inches by 2 ½ inches by 2 inches thick. I find air-dried wood carves more cleanly than kiln-dried. Make sure the grain runs lengthwise for strength.

Trace or photocopy the pattern in the book and cut around the outline to make a template. Place the template on the block of wood and draw around the outline with a pencil.

Next, cut the blank with a band saw or coping saw.

After the blank is cut out, draw some guidelines on the blank with pencil. These are just rough lines to help you visualize the shape that you will be carving into the wood.

Begin carving by rounding off all the sharp corners with a carving knife. Don't worry about carving off your guidelines. They can be redrawn later as you need them.

At this stage of the carving you can remove quite a lot of wood to give St. Nicholas a rounded shape. Don't worry about taking off too much. In twenty years of teaching, I have found this almost never happens. It is more common to leave too much wood on and end up with a square or blocky carving.

After the carving is rounded, carve a notch no more than $\frac{1}{8}$ inch deep underneath the arms and fur cuffs on the sleeves. This is a two-step procedure that separates the sleeves from the bottom part of the robe.

First, use the paring cut to cut in at a 45-degree angle.

Then, use the levering cut to make another cut at a 45-degree angle from the opposite direction.

Those two cuts meet at the bottom to remove a clean chip.

Don't try to remove all the wood at once. It is easier to repeat the notching step two or three times, deepening the cut each time. You also run less risk of splitting the wood this way.

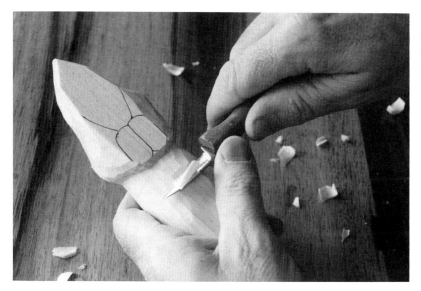

After the notch is cut, pare away the excess wood below it to smooth the bottom of the robe.

Then, round the arms above the notch.

Sketch in pencil lines showing Santa's belt and the fur trim at the bottom of his robe. Both the belt and the trim are about ¼ inch wide.

You can make shallow notches along these lines with your knife using the same technique you used to create the notch under the arms.

Or you can use a small 3mm no. 12 V-gouge to incise a line $\frac{1}{16}$ inch deep. The V-gouge is one of the most useful tools in a carver's collection. It is simply a gouge with a V-shaped cutting edge. It can form a notch with one cut and is very helpful for creating fine details on a carving.

However, it can be a tricky tool to sharpen. Before you use it, test it for sharpness, and if necessary touch up the cutting edge. The V-gouge won't cut well unless it is perfectly sharp.

If you are unfamiliar with the techniques for safely using gouges, please refer to the instructions in "Getting Started."

Remember to brace the fingers of the hand holding the tool against the carving for safety and stability. And keep the fingers of the hand holding the carving out of the path of the tool in case it slips.

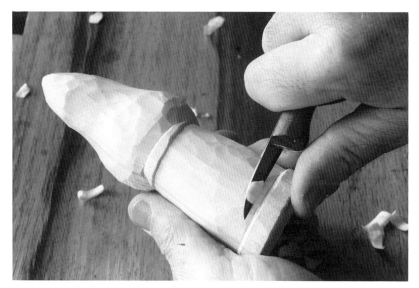

Use your knife to pare away the wood above and below the belt, leaving it raised. Use the same technique to remove the wood above the fur trim at the bottom of the robe.

To help create the illusion of soft fur, round the sharp edges on the fur trim.

Next, round the top of the hood. This St. Nicholas's hood slopes from a peak at the back toward the face like a medieval monk's cowl.

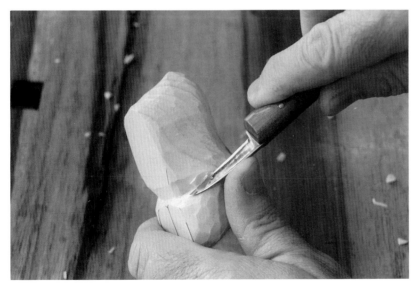

Now, to form the top of the arms, make a notch above the fur cuffs on the sleeves and extending partway around the sides.

With your carving knife, round the sleeves and fur cuffs.

Sketch the outlines of the fur cuffs on the sleeves and outline them with the 3mm V-gouge. I am holding the tool in the pencil grip. The fingers of my right hand, which holds the gouge, are braced against the wood, and the fingers of my left hand are out of the path of the tool for safety.

Then, use the knife to bevel the excess wood on the sleeves, leaving the cuffs raised.

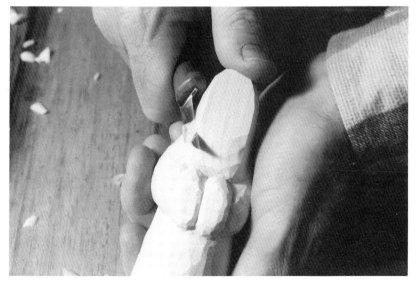

To prepare for shaping the face, pare the sides of the hood down so the shapes flow smoothly from the hood to the sleeves of the robe.

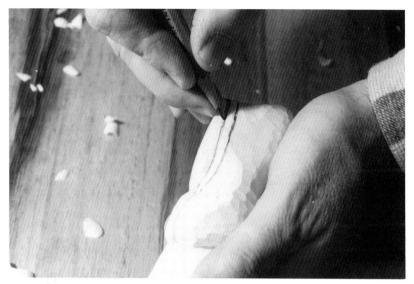

Next, pencil in the lines for the fur trim on the hood. The trim here is slightly less than ¼ inch wide. Notice that the hood is set about ¼ inch back from the face area. This will give you room to carve the face details.

Use the V-gouge to incise along both outer edges of the fur trim. Then, pare away the excess wood on the face area and the hood leaving the trim raised. This is the same technique used to create the cuffs on the sleeves.

Then, gently round off the sharp edges of the trim.

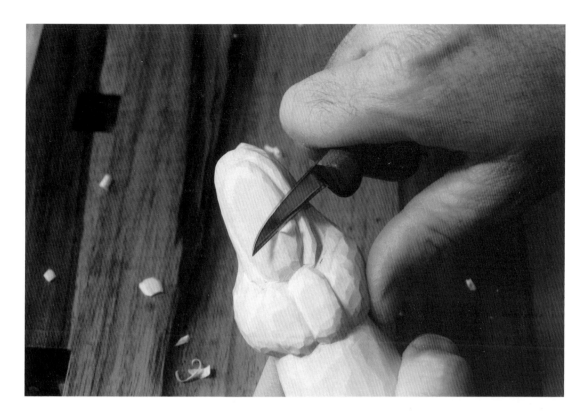

The final step in preparation for doing the face is to round off the sides of the face, forehead area, and beard.

After these are rounded, lightly pencil in some guidelines for carving the face. Draw a horizontal line across the face ⅜ inch down from the top to mark where the eyes will be carved. Draw a second line ⅜ inch below the first to form the bottom of the nose and cheeks.

Before you actually begin carving the face, take a minute to check your tools for sharpness. The secret of a crisply carved face is a knife that is razor sharp right to the tip.

You will notice from the photographs that I have switched to a finer, more pointed detailing knife for the face. Although you can use your regular carving knife, the fine point will make carving the details easier.

I also find it helpful to use a low-power magnifying visor when I work on faces. It enlarges the tiny details and helps me make precise cuts.

Use the knife to carve two notches $\frac{1}{8}$ inch deep where you drew the lines. The lines mark the center of the notch.

If you look at the face from the front at this point, it doesn't seem to bear much resemblance to a human face. Turn the carving sideways, however, and look at St. Nicholas's profile. You can see the nose and forehead plainly.

These two notches determine the proportions of the face, and you can create different expressions by varying them. If the two notches are close together, your carving will have a short "pug" nose. If they are farther apart, the nose will be longer.

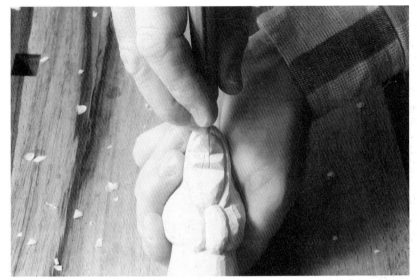

To create St. Nicholas's nose, hold the knife in the pencil grip and carefully incise two vertical lines forming the sides of the nose. Notice that the fingers of the hand holding the knife are braced against the carving for extra stability and safety.

Then, pare away the excess wood over the cheeks, leaving the nose raised.

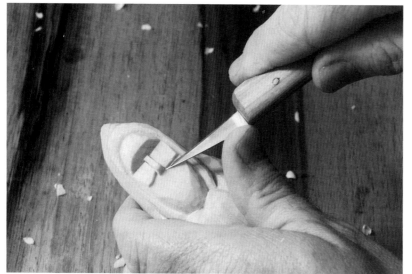

Now, remove a tiny triangular chip from each cheek at the base of the nose. Cut down vertically to form the sides of the chip and remove it with a horizontal cut.

A knife with a straight cutting edge is especially helpful here because you always know exactly where the point of the knife is inside the wood. Practice helps too. It gives you a sense of how to make three cuts that meet precisely, and remove a clean chip.

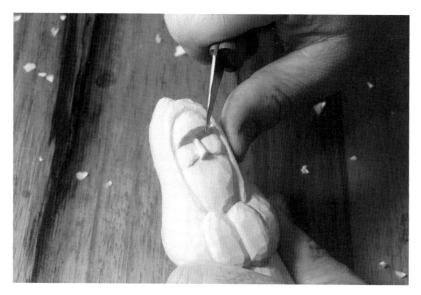

Then, round off the sharp angles on the cheeks, forehead, and nose. This is a rather delicate step, so remove the wood slowly, in paper-thin shavings.

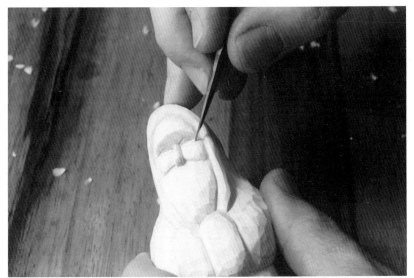

Now, you are ready for the eyes. Hold the knife in the pencil grip and very carefully incise a line 1/32 inch deep around the outline of the eye. Try to hold the knife perpendicular to the surface of the wood when you make these cuts.

Then, remove a paper-thin shaving above and below the eye, leaving it raised. This forms the eyeball.

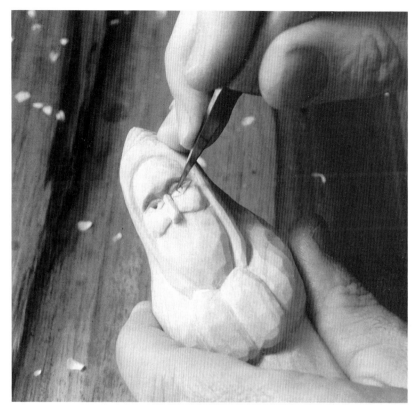

To make a pupil, remove a tiny triangular chip from the lower half of the eye with the point of your knife. Make sure the pupils are in the same place on both eyes. You don't want a cross-eyed St. Nicholas.

This technique produces a carved eye that is actually a simplified interpretation of a real human eye. But it gives a more lifelike effect on a carving of this scale. The aim on a small carving is to create the illusion of detail from a normal viewing distance. Too many details on a small carving make it look fussy and overworked.

St. Nicholas's full mustache is created the same way the eyelids are. First, hold the knife in the pencil grip and incise a line about $1/32$ inch deep along the lower edge of the mustache. Then, pare away a thin shaving below the mustache, leaving it raised.

I always enjoy this stage of a carving. It almost seems like magic when suddenly you have a little person looking back at you.

When the face is carved, you can move on to the finishing details. Use a small V-gouge to texture St. Nicholas's hair, beard, and mustache and the fur trim on his robe. It helps to experiment on a piece of scrap wood before you start. This will give you a feeling for the different textures that can be created with this simple tool.

I used long, flowing strokes for the beard to give it a soft, silky look. For the trim I used short strokes about $1/8$ inch long to create a dense, fluffy fur texture.

This is the finished carving before painting.

I painted this carving green in the European St. Nicholas tradition. Whatever color you choose, the key to painting a small figure like this is subtlety. The colors should be soft and transparent to let the wood grain show through slightly. The only exception to this is the white I used for the hair, beard, and fur trim. For these I prefer titanium white acrylic. Acrylic paint is more opaque than oil paint and covers the wood better.

Thin the paint slightly with water for a nice, creamy brushing consistency. You don't want the paint too thick or it will fill in some of the texture you carved on the trim and beard.

Use a small pointed brush, such as a no. 2 synthetic sable, for this step. I recommend buying good quality brushes and caring for them meticulously. A good brush gives you better control in painting and will give years of service if it is cleaned gently and completely. Never let paint dry on a brush. Even if you manage to work the dried paint out, the texture of the brush will be ruined.

After the white paint has dried thoroughly, about fifteen to twenty minutes, paint the rest of the carving with oil paints thinned with turpentine or mineral spirits to a transparent stain. I am using a no. 1 China bristle brush for this step. Oil paints are more transparent than acrylics and give a warm, natural look to the carving. I used phthalo green, a woodsy color similar to that used on many traditional German folk carvings.

You may want to experiment with alkyd paints instead of oils. They handle just like oil paints and can be thinned with turpentine or mineral spirits, but they dry in hours instead of days. Winsor & Newton is one company that makes a line of alkyd paints.

You can leave the face the natural wood color or you can tint it very softly. Use a mixture of burnt umber and burnt sienna thinned almost water-clear with turpentine or mineral spirits. This should be the palest possible wash of transparent color. Test the color on a scrap of the same type of wood you are carving. Make it just dark enough to add a hint of warmth to the natural wood color.

You can also give St. Nicholas rosy cheeks by dry brushing on the faintest blush of cadmium red medium. I find the best way to do this is to put a small dab of red paint on a white piece of paper. Dip the tip of a fine, pointed sable brush into the paint, then brush it nearly dry on the white paper. When you are leaving just a hint of color on the paper, gently brush some onto the cheeks. My rule of thumb is to stop when I think I am about half done.

As a historical note, this type of painting with transparent stains is called tinting. It can be seen on many old carvings in museums and private collections.

For a final detail, you can add a pattern of small gold dots to St. Nicholas's robe. Let the carving dry overnight before painting the dots on.

I used Testor's gold enamel for this step. It is available in ¼-ounce jars in hobby shops. Enamels have great covering power and add a touch of shine.

This type of St. Nicholas woodcarving is really fun to make. You may find yourself carving several of them for friends and family. At first it may seem challenging, but as your skills develop, you will find each one becomes easier to carve.

Adirondack Santa

MY HOME IS IN THE ADIRONDACKS OF NORTHERN New York State. This region is a mountainous wilderness preserve of more than six million acres, many times larger than most of our national parks.

The harsh climate and difficulties of traveling kept this region virtually unexplored until after the rest of the United States had been settled. It was only during the later half of the nineteenth century that a few hardy people began to live here on a permanent, year-round basis. Even the native Indians didn't stay through the long winters, which shows they had more sense than the rest of us.

The first Adirondack inhabitants were lumberjacks, a few hopeful farmers, and the occasional hermit. As more families began to settle in the small lakeside villages, a regional image of Santa Claus developed—much as it has in other rural mountain areas.

I believe it began when Swedish lumberjacks told children stories of the "Tomten," small, shy people who lived in the forest. They were friends of the animals and watched over the forest and farms. During the Christmas season, they traveled from house to house bringing gifts for the children and treats for the wildlife and farm animals.

Other people told stories around the evening fire of a magical hermit, a friend of the forest animals who lived deep in the woods. On Christmas Eve he would travel throughout the village with his companion, an Adirondack black bear, and bring children gifts of fruit and handmade wooden toys.

As with any Christmas legend, the message of peace and kindness to all brought warmth to people's hearts during the long winter months.

Carving the Adirondack Santa is very similar in technique to the first project in this book. The main difference is that I added a few details that were carved separately. I carved the packs for Santa and his bear from pine scraps and then textured the sides for detailing. The real Adirondack pack baskets, still used by local guides, are woven from ash wood splints.

Again, carving the face may seem like a challenge. Just make sure your knife is sharp and take it step by step, and you won't have any problems.

Carving the bear is also fairly straightforward, and I don't think you will have any great difficulty. The packages in the pack can either be carved in place, which is excellent practice, or carved separately and glued in.

White pine is my first choice for this project. It seems appropriate because the forests around my home are full of beautiful white-pine trees.

If you can't find good air-dried white pine, basswood will work too. You will need a piece 5 1/2 inches by 2 1/2 inches by 2 inches, plus some scraps for the pack basket and snowshoes.

ADIRONDACK SANTA

Tools

Carving knife
Detail knife
35mm no. 1 gouge
12mm no. 23 macaroni gouge
8mm no. 12 V-gouge
3mm no. 12 V-gouge
3mm no. 11 veiner
Woodburning pen
Paintbrushes
Drill with 1/8-inch bit

Materials

Air-dried white pine or basswood
    5 1/2 inches by 2 1/2 inches by 2
      inches
Quick-set epoxy glue
Acrylic paint
    titanium white
Oil or alkyd paint
    burnt umber
    burnt sienna
    cadmium red medium
    raw sienna
    viridian green
    black
Enamel paint
    red
    green
    gold

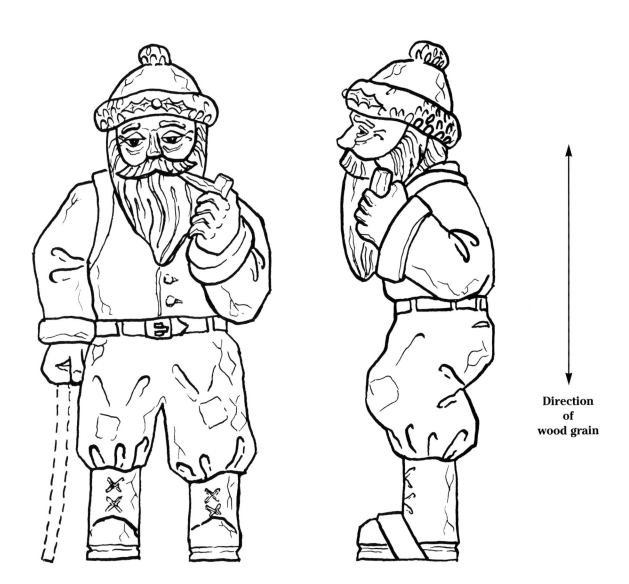

Direction of wood grain

**Direction
of
wood grain**

To begin the Adirondack Santa, cut the side view out on the band saw.

Next, trace the front view pattern on the back of the blank. This way the carving will be face down on the band-saw table when you cut it out. The front side of the blank is the flattest; it will be easier and safer to cut it out resting on this side.

Before you begin carving, pencil in some rough guidelines showing where the arms are in relation to the body, and where the beard will be.

You can use a knife to rough out this carving as we did with the Alpine St. Nicholas, or you can use gouges to remove the excess wood in the beginning stages. If you use gouges, fasten the blank securely to your workbench. For safety, keep both hands on the gouge and always carve away from yourself. Remember, any tool sizes and shapes that I mention are only suggestions. Feel free to substitute, using the gouges you already have on hand.

Begin by using a large, flat gouge, such as a 35mm no. 1, to round off the sharp angles on the legs. You will notice that I have fastened the carving to the bench using bench dogs. Because the feet are cross grain and somewhat fragile, I put an extra block of wood under them. It goes between the carving and the bench dog to give the feet extra support and protection while they are clamped in the vise.

Then, use a 12mm macaroni gouge to rough out the arms and outline the beard.

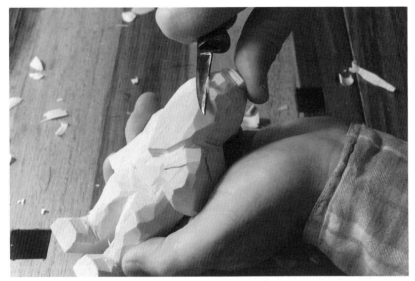

After the carving has been roughed out with the gouges, remove it from the bench and use your carving knife to round off the sharp angles.

Next, shape the feet. Remember, the toes are cross grain, so don't put too much pressure on them as you carve. If they do split off at some point, just glue them back on. Any good wood glue, like Elmer's or Titebond, will do. Just give it time to cure before you go back to carving. Follow the manufacturer's instructions for curing time.

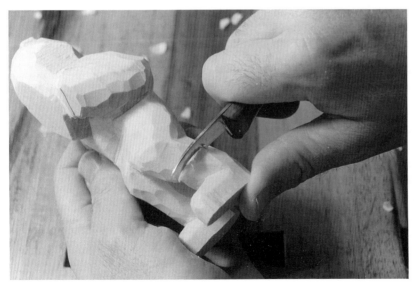

An authentic Adirondack Santa always wears his heavy wool pants tucked into his boots to keep snow out. Make a notch around the bottom of the pants legs by cutting down at a 45-degree angle to make the first side of the notch.

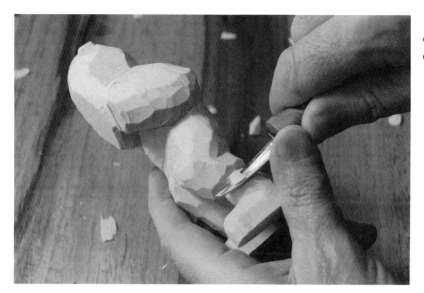

Then, make a cut in from the opposite direction to remove a clean chip.

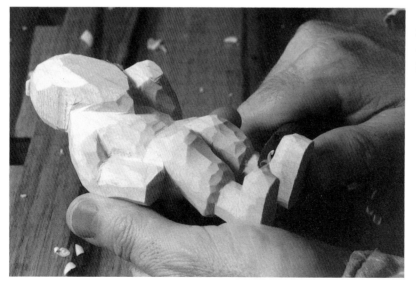

Shape the boot, making it narrower than the pants leg to create the illusion that the pants leg is tucked into it.

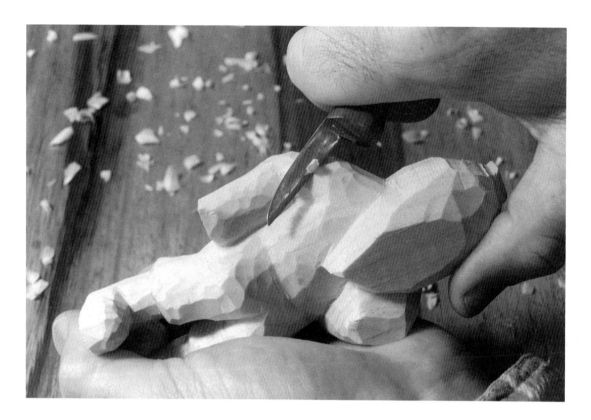

Next, shape the right arm. Round off the sharp angles and be sure to leave plenty of wood for the cuff and hand. An Adirondack Santa wears a heavy coat, so don't make the arm too thin.

Before you begin carving the cuff, pencil in some guidelines. The cuff is ¼ inch wide, and its lower edge is ½ inch above the end of the arm. Use a medium-size V-gouge, like an 8mm no. 12, to incise along the lines you have drawn.

For safety, be sure to brace the fingers of the hand holding the gouge against the wood. As always, keep your other hand out of the way of the tool in case it slips.

Keep these cuts shallow, no more than $\frac{1}{16}$ inch deep. Then, use your carving knife to pare down the wood above and below the cuff, leaving it raised.

The right hand is carved in the shape of a closed fist to hold a walking stock. When I carve hands, I find it helps to use my own as a model. Put your hand in the same position as the carving's and study the basic shapes. Don't worry about details at this point; just look at the broad planes of the form.

Keep the shapes simple. A closed fist is basically boxlike with a little extra wood left on one side to allow for the thumb.

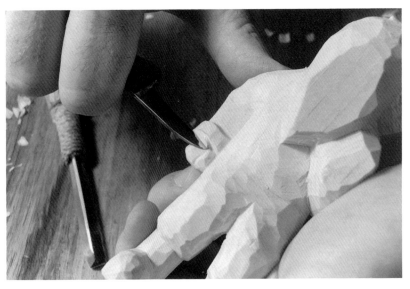

To form the fingers and thumb, make a few simple lines with the V-gouge. First, outline the edge of the thumb. Then, with your knife, pare away a little wood on the front of the hand to make the thumb stand out.

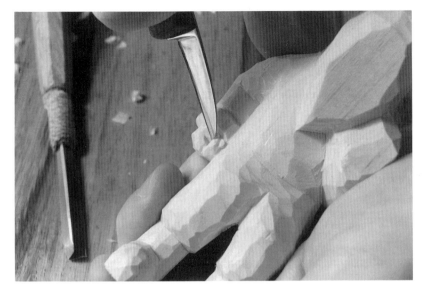

Next, remove a tiny triangular chip from the hand next to the thumb to help create the illusion of curled fingers.

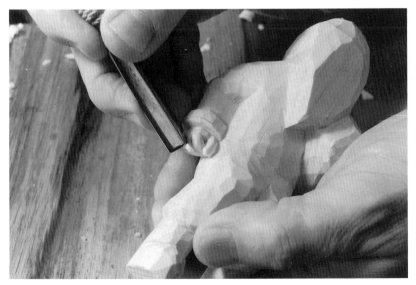

Now, pencil in three lines to indicate the spaces between the fingers. Use the V-gouge to incise shallow cuts along these lines to form the fingers.

Santa's left hand is curled loosely into a fist by his shoulder to hold the pipe. Begin by rounding off the sharp angles.

Then, pencil in a line showing the separation between the forearm and the shoulder. Make a cut along this line with the V-gouge. Finally, use the knife to pare away the excess wood on either side of the cut to round the arm and shoulder.

Pencil in the cuff, making it $\frac{1}{4}$ inch wide and $\frac{1}{2}$ inch from the end of the arm. Outline the cuff with the V-gouge, making the cuts only about $\frac{1}{16}$ inch deep.

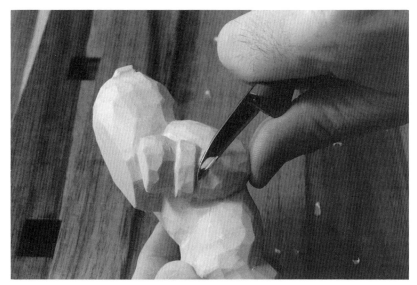

Carve off the excess wood on the hand and arm, leaving the cuff raised.

When shaping the hand, carve the bold shapes first, then the details, such as the fingers. Once again, it is a big help to put your hand in the same position as Santa's and look at the shapes in a mirror. Getting a friend to model for you helps, too.

Shape the hand with the carving knife. With the V-gouge, cut a groove in the top of the fist to separate the thumb from the fingers. This also forms a slight hollow to fit the pipe into.

Then incise three lines on the hand to form the fingers. Because of the limited clearance between the hand and the beard, I am using a smaller 3mm no. 12 V-gouge for this step.

The next step in making the Adirondack Santa is carving the face. Begin by rounding off the sharp angles on the whole top of the head, including the pompom on the hat. Don't worry about any details at this point; they will be handled later.

Lightly pencil in guidelines showing the fur trim on the hat, a centerline down the middle of the face, and the outline of the beard.

Make a horizontal line ¼ inch down from the edge of the hat to mark the position of the eyes, and another ¼ inch below it marking the bottom of the nose.

With the V-gouge, incise around the fur trim of the hat. Then pare away the wood above and below the trim, leaving it raised. After this step you will have to redraw some of the guidelines for the face.

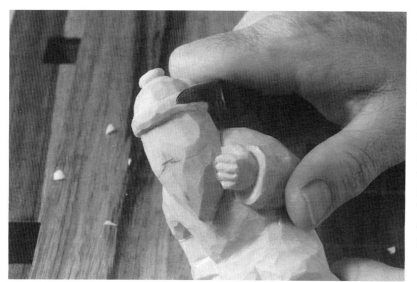

Round the edges of the trim to make it appear softer.

You can use your regular carving knife for the face, but I have found that a detail knife with an extrafine point makes it easier to control the cuts. Whichever knife you use, just be sure that it is razor sharp to the very tip. If your knife is dull, the face will look crude and "fuzzy." The cuts have to be perfectly crisp and clean to create a life-like effect.

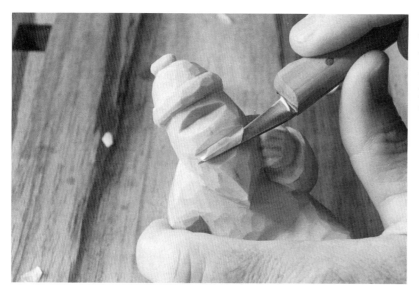

With the knife, carefully cut two notches ⅛ inch deep along the two horizontal lines you have drawn across the face. The lines you have drawn indicate the deepest part of the cut.

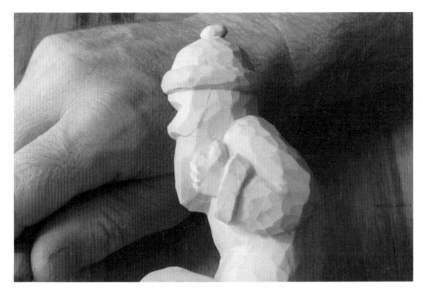

Now, shape the wood between the two notches to create the profile of the nose. I gave this Santa a slightly turned-up nose.

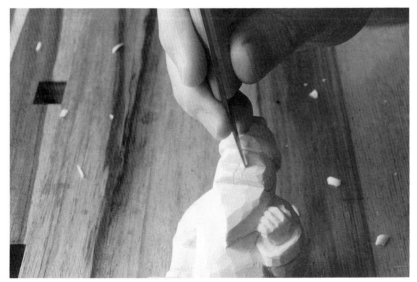

Looking at the face from the front, make two vertical cuts, no more than $\frac{1}{8}$ inch deep, to form the sides of the nose. The cuts should be $\frac{1}{8}$ inch apart at the base and taper slightly closer together toward the bridge.

Then, gently pare away the cheeks, leaving the nose raised. Don't try to remove all the wood at once; pare it away in a series of thin shavings to avoid taking too much off. Don't round or shape the cheeks at this point. It works better to wait until the beard is shaped.

You can leave the nose just as it looks now, or you can very carefully remove a thin shaving from each side to round off the corners, giving it a more realistic shape.

To make the bottom of the cheeks look rounded, remove the tiny triangular chip from each cheek at the base of the nose. Cut down vertically with the point of the knife to form the sides of the chip, then remove it with a small horizontal cut.

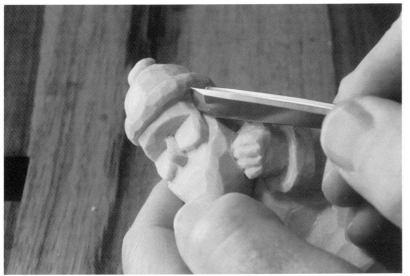

The next step is to shape the beard. Use the 8mm V-gouge to carefully incise a line separating the face and the beard. Pare away some wood on the cheek side of your V cut to smooth the tool marks and establish the width of the face. Then, round the beard side of the cut to make the beard look softer and more flowing. These steps make the face stand clear of the beard and give it definition.

Next, round the cheeks. Remove only thin shavings, leaving plenty of wood to give the cheeks a plump, cheery look.

Check your knife for sharpness before you start the eyes. I usually strop my knife lightly at this point, just to make sure it is razor sharp.

Begin by holding the knife in the pencil grip and outlining the eyes. Make the cut only about $\frac{1}{32}$ inch deep. Be sure to hold the knife perpendicular to the surface of the wood when making these cuts.

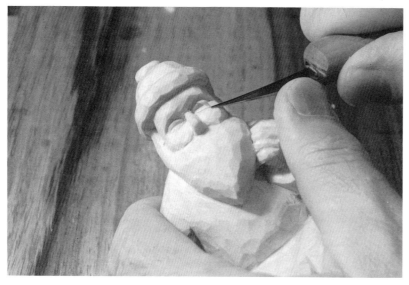

Next, remove a paper-thin shaving above and below the eyelids, leaving them slightly raised.

To make the pupil of Santa's eye, remove a tiny triangular chip of wood from the lower half of the eye. Although the pupil of an eye is actually round, on a carving of this size a triangular cut gives more sparkle and expression. Before you begin this cut, check the position of the pupils. You want to be sure both eyes are looking in the same direction.

Use the very tip of your knife to make three small cuts angled in so they meet at the bottom, removing a clean chip.

To create wrinkles under Santa's eyes, use the same basic technique you used to make the eyelids. Hold the knife in the pencil grip and incise a very shallow line into the cheek below the eye. Hold the blade perpendicular to the wood. Don't cut into the wood at an angle or the wrinkle will be undercut and will break off, leaving a rough surface.

Remove a paper-thin shaving below the cut to create the wrinkle.

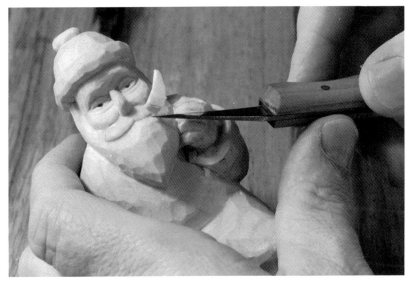

After the eyes are done, pencil in Santa's shaggy mustache. Use the same techniques as you did to create the eye to make the mustache. Incise a line a little more than 1/32 inch deep along the lower edge of the mustache. Then, pare away the beard below the mustache.

Once you have finished the face, you have the trickiest part of the carving behind you. Now comes the fun part: adding the finishing touches that give the carving character and personality.

An optional touch I like is a sprig of holly on Santa's cap. Sketch the leaves and berries on lightly, then outline them with a small V-gouge, such as the 3mm no. 12.

To make the fur trim look soft and fluffy, texture it by making short cuts with a V-gouge or a small veiner, such as a 3mm no. 11. A veiner is a gouge with a U-shaped cutting edge. Using this tool helps create the illusion of softness on the fur trim because it makes a rounded cut rather than a sharply angled one.

For Santa's beard, mustache, and hair I use the 3mm V-gouge because it creates a finer texture. Make long, curving cuts so the beard looks soft and flowing.

Next, sketch in the pack basket straps and the belt, making them both about ⅛ inch wide. Outline the straps with the small V-gouge. Keep the cuts shallow: the belt and straps need to be raised only a tiny fraction of an inch above the level of the wool shirt to create the right effect.

After outlining, pare away the excess wood with the carving knife.

After the belt and straps are finished, you are ready to start the boots. Pencil in lines to indicate the snowshoe straps and the sole of the boot. Outline the straps with the small V-gouge and pare away the excess wood. Incise a line along the bottom edge of the boot to make the sole. Be careful not to cut through the snowshoe straps; they go over the whole boot.

If you like, you can make one or two small Xs with the V-gouge on the ankle of the boot to suggest laces. To make a heel, just remove a small triangular chip from the bottom of the boots.

For the snowshoes I used two pieces of scrap wood $\frac{1}{4}$ inch thick and whittled them to shape with my knife. Then I sanded them smooth with 220 grit garnet paper.

The best way to create the texture of the leather lacing is to lightly scorch it in with a fine woodburning pen. I use a Detail Master II with a skew tip (1-C).

This Santa carries his toys in an Adirondack pack basket. These baskets were hand woven of ash splints. Guides and hermits used them over a century ago to carry heavy loads. A few craftsmen still make them by hand today. They are unsurpassed for carrying fragile or oddly shaped items that a cloth backpack can't handle.

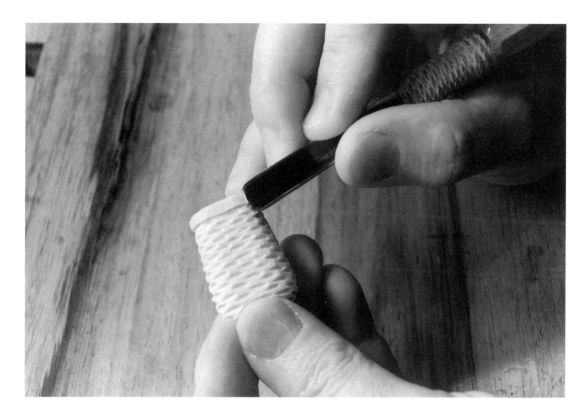

Whittle the basic shape from a scrap of white pine about 1 1/2 inch by 1 inch by 1 inch. Then use the 8mm no. 12 V-gouge to make a series of short cuts that suggest the woven ash splints. To make a better gluing surface, leave a small flat area on the side that touches Santa's back.

If you like, you can whittle some small items that poke out the top of Santa's pack basket. I whittled a small evergreen tree out of a scrap of 3/8-inch-thick pine. The basic shape is like a series of cones, one on top of the other. I cut off the bottom cone at an angle, leaving a small peg of wood to fit into a 1/8-inch hole drilled into the top of the pack basket.

For added detail you can texture the evergreen with the 3mm no. 11 veiner. When carving a piece this small, work slowly and carefully. You don't need a lot of force to remove these small chips.

To give Santa a walking stick, drill a ⅛-inch-wide hole at least ¼ inch deep into the bottom of the right hand. I angled the hole slightly toward the body so that the walking stick will slant outward a bit and clear the snowshoes.

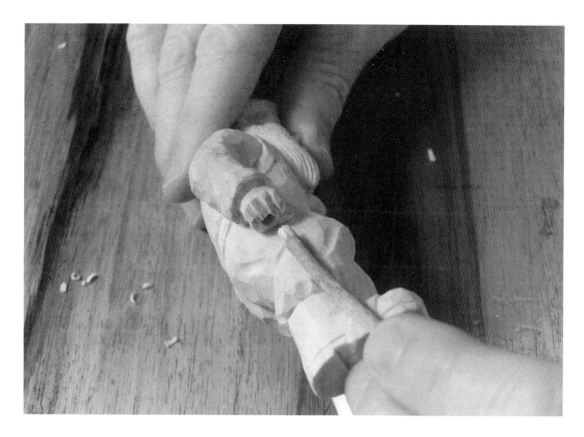

Find or whittle a twig slightly longer than necessary and test fit it into the hole. I don't recommend gluing the walking stick in or cutting it to the exact length until the carving is painted and the snowshoes are glued on.

Whittle a pipe from a piece of scrap wood and test fit it in Santa's hand. If necessary, adjust the shape of the stem and bowl to the pipe fits neatly in the hand and tucks up under the edge of the mustache. You may have to make a tiny groove in the beard with the small V-gouge to fit the pipe stem in properly.

Don't glue the pipe in at this point. Set it aside in a safe place so it won't get lost in the chips on your workbench. Believe me, I've learned this step the hard way!

Before you begin painting, test fit the pack basket onto Santa's back. Circle a small area on the back and the pack basket where the two will be glued together. Don't apply paint in these areas; it will weaken the glue bond.

Start by painting Santa's hair, beard, mustache, and the fur trim and tassel on his cap white. I use titanium white acrylic paint for this step. Acrylic paint is water-based and dries quickly. It also has good covering power and gives a truer white for this stage of the painting. If you carved holly on the cap, paint right over it with the white acrylic, which will make a good base coat to paint color on later.

As an optional detail, you can use a very fine paintbrush, such as a no. 1 sable, to paint Santa's eyebrows and lower eyelids white.

Be careful not to get any paint inside the triangular chip that forms the pupil of the eye. The dark shadow inside the chip is what gives the eye its lifelike appearance.

Paint the beard before gluing in the pipe to make staining the pipe easier. If white paint from the beard gets on the pipe it is difficult to clean off. However, the transparent oil stain we will be using on the pipe and the rest of the carving is easy to wipe off the acrylic paint of the beard.

After the white paint is dry, glue the pipe on with a quick-setting epoxy, such as Duro Master Mend Epoxy Quick Set. I like a fast-setting epoxy for this step because you can hold the pipe in the proper position while the glue sets, usually within five or six minutes.

If you like, you can also glue the snowshoes on at this time. Before you glue, make sure the bottoms of Santa's boots and the bottoms of the snowshoes are flat so that the carving stands level.

Test first. If you notice any tippiness, sand the bottom of the boots with 180 grit sandpaper until the carving stands level.

After I painted Santa's beard and glued on his pipe and snowshoes, I decided to add one last touch to the carving. I put a couple of patches on Santa's pants. Like most of the other details, these were carved by simply outlining them with the 3mm V-gouge, then paring away a little wood around the outline cuts.

After the white acrylic paint is completely dry, you can finish painting the carving. I used alkyd paints thinned to a transparent stain with paint thinner. This creates a soft, natural effect that lets the wood grain show through.

The colors I use are only suggestions. Feel free to substitute, using whatever colors you prefer.

For the face, use a very light mixture of burnt umber and burnt sienna. Make this color very dilute. When you can just barely see it on the test block, the color is right.

To add rosy cheeks take a tiny amount of cadmium red medium on a small brush and make test strokes on a pad of white paper. When the brush leaves a barely visible whisper of color on the pad, carefully dry-brush a little onto Santa's cheeks. A good rule of thumb is to stop when you have applied about half as much paint as you think you need. This is enough to add a hint of warmth to Santa's face. Don't overdo this step—too bright a red will make Santa look garish.

Burnt umber makes a nice, warm brown for the pipe, boots, belt, and pack basket.

To make a subtle contrasting color for the pack straps and snowshoes, use a lighter shade of burnt umber with just a little raw sienna added to make a golden brown.

I used cadmium red medium for the shirt. Because this is a very intense color, I dilute it with enough thinner to create a soft, slightly weathered red.

The pants traditionally worn in the Adirondacks are thick, densely woven wool trousers in muted grays or greens. They are naturally water resistant and so durable that they are often passed down as heirlooms from one generation to the next.

The trousers were woven locally in mill towns in the foothills of the Adirondack mountain range. They were usually referred to as "Malone pants" or "Warrensburgh's" after the towns where they were made.

Viridian green and burnt umber make a muted forest green that works well for the trousers and wool cap. If you carved patches on the pants, first paint the pants completely. Then, add a little more burnt umber to the basic green to darken the patches.

Use viridian green on the small evergreen tree for Santa's pack. Leave the peg at the bottom unpainted so that the glue will adhere to it better.

For very tiny details, like the holly and belt buckle, I used Testor's gloss enamel. Enamels are paints with good covering power and a hint of shine. They are available in hobby shops in tiny $\frac{1}{4}$-ounce jars. I used red and green for the holly and gold for the belt buckle.

To give Santa a traditional plaid shirt, first let the red paint dry overnight. If the red paint is not dry, the black paint will spread or bleed into the red areas.

Dilute the black paint with turpentine or mineral spirits until the color is a weak, faded black. Too intense a black will look harsh and unnatural. Diluting the color gives Santa's shirt a soft, weathered look.

Use a no. 3 sable brush. To get the right effect, dip the brush into the paint and make practice strokes on a piece of scrap wood until some of the paint is absorbed from the brush and you can control the width of the line easily.

Then paint horizontal and vertical lines on the shirt to suggest a plaid fabric. You could look at a plaid shirt to get a feeling for how the stripes run, but don't worry about making it too exact. As I've mentioned before, on a carving of this scale, it is better to suggest detail than to try and put it all in. Many woven plaids are very complex; to try to dupli-cate them exactly would be frus-trating and actually detract from the realism of the carving. Besides, as anyone who is famil-iar with the mountains knows, traditional Adirondack clothing tends to have a certain haphaz-ard charm.

If you like a slightly weathered look, you can *very lightly* sand the carving with 280 grit garnet or aluminum oxide sandpaper, after the paint is completely dry. Just make one or two gentle passes over the surface. This removes a little bit of the paint from the ridges left by the tool marks and gives the carving a slightly aged appearance.

Use a light hand for this step and stop when you see the paint lighten in the raised areas. Too much pressure could round off the tool marks and spoil the hand-carved appearance.

Next, dry fit the walking stick into Santa's hand and carefully cut it off to the right length. Glue it in with quick-set epoxy, holding it in the right position until the glue sets.

At this point you can also glue the small evergreen tree into the pack basket and fasten the basket to Santa's back.

Now that the carving is finished, you can leave it as it is or you can add a light protective finish of paste wax.

Apply the wax with a soft rag or a small bristle brush. Then buff gently with a clean horse-hair shoe brush. A thin coat is best; if applied too heavily, solvents in the wax will dissolve oil paints and enamels.

Paste wax protects the wood and gives it a soft, natural glow. It will also allow the carving to darken slightly with age, adding warmth and character.

Adirondack Santa's Bear

ACCORDING TO LOCAL LEGENDS THE ADIRONDACK Santa Claus is always accompanied by his faithful companion, a black bear. The bear helps carry presents and even Christmas trees to deserving children and their families.

Older folks would tell stories of how the bear sometimes pulled Santa's sleigh through the deep winter snow, much like the Russian legends of Grandfather Frost and his bear.

To make the Adirondack Santa's black bear, use a piece of 2-inch-thick air-dried white pine or basswood 3 inches by 5 inches. The grain should run the length of the body, nose to tail, for added strength and easy carving.

ADIRONDACK SANTA'S BEAR

Tools

Coping saw
30mm no. 2 gouge
3mm no. 12 V-gouge
8mm no. 8 gouge
Paintbrushes

Materials

Air-dried white pine or basswood
    3 inches by 5 inches by 2 inches
Quick-set epoxy glue
Oil or alkyd paint
    yellow ochre
    burnt umber
    black
    raw sienna
    cadmium red medium
    viridian green
Enamel paint
    red
    gold
    white

Direction of wood grain

Cut the profile view out on the band saw. Sketch the outlines of the legs on the bear. Mark the forelegs clearly, showing which is the right and which is the left.

Clamp the blank in a vise and cut down between the legs with a coping saw. Make two cuts to form a slot about ¼ inch wide in the center of the bear blank. Stop cutting just before the saw touches the stomach. These saw cuts will make it much easier to clear out the wood between the legs.

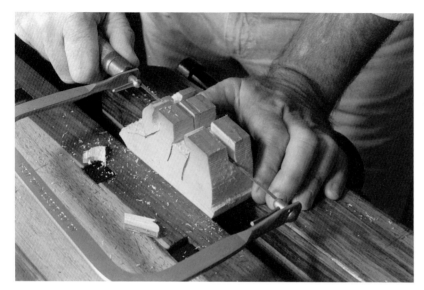

One of the advantages of the coping saw is that the blade is narrow enough to turn sideways. Turn the blade and make a horizontal cut removing the waste wood between the legs.

Next, turn the bear sideways and fasten it to the bench. Use a large gouge with a shallow sweep, like a 3mm no. 2, to remove the excess wood, leaving you with one right leg and one left leg. You can also carve the wood away with a knife, but a gouge is more efficient.

While the bear is fastened to the bench and you have the large gouge handy you can remove more of the excess wood. Make two vertical cuts, one behind the front leg and one in front of the hind leg.

Then use the gouge to shave away some of the wood between the two cuts. This rounds the stomach.

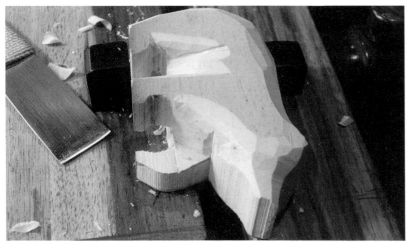

Use the gouge to round off the sharp angles on the body and narrow the bear's head slightly.

Now, remove the bear from the bench. Most of the remaining work will be done with a carving knife.

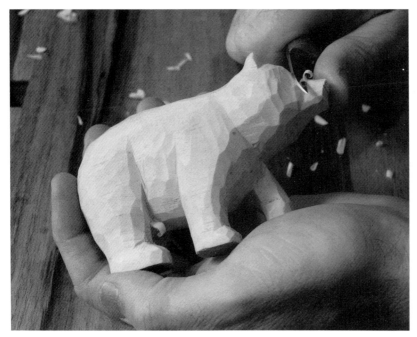

A bear, especially in the winter, has a thick layer of fat and very heavy fur. So, the basic shape is roly-poly without a lot of detail. With your carving knife, simply round off all the sharp angles on the body and legs, and roughly shape the face and ears.

To make the tail, just outline it with a V-gouge and pare away the excess wood.

Next, shape the muzzle. Work slowly and take off small chips. Small changes in the shape of the face can make a big change in the bear's expression, so be careful not to take off too much wood at once.

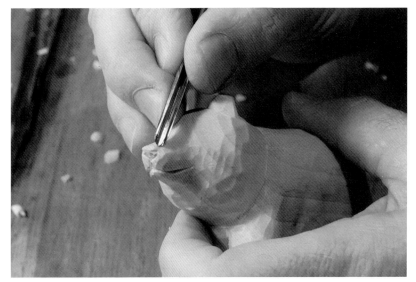

After the muzzle is shaped, pencil in the lines for the mouth. Use a 3mm no. 12 V-gouge to incise the lines. Make sure your V-gouge is perfectly sharp because you are carving on end grain.

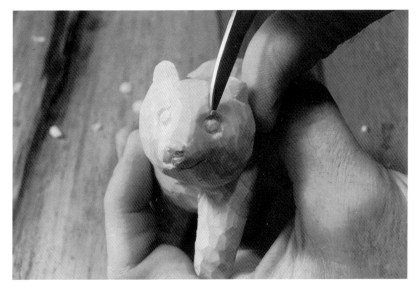

For the eyes, pencil in a circle marking the position. Then, with a small V-gouge, carefully incise a circle around the eyes. Round off the eyeball inside the circle to make the eye look more realistic.

To finish the ears, hollow them slightly with a gouge like an 8mm no. 8.

To texture the bear's fur, make short, scooping cuts with your knife to suggest a shaggy coat.

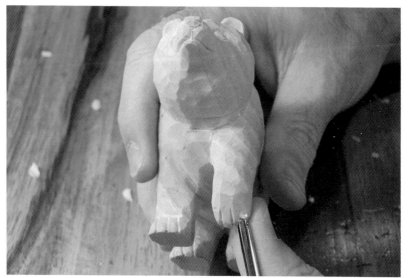

For the toes, incise three lines on each foot with the V-gouge.

To make the collar, incise two very shallow lines around the neck with the small V-gouge. These lines do not need to be carved deeply; they mainly serve as painting guides.

As an option you can carve two small Adirondack pack baskets for the bear to carry. These are carved the same way Santa's pack basket is.

If you like, you can leave a little extra wood at the top shaped like wrapped Christmas presents. Carve a pack strap around the bear's middle the same way you carved the collar. Test fit the pack baskets and hollow out the backs slightly to adjust the fit to the curve of the bear.

Don't glue the pack baskets on until after the bear is painted. With a pencil, mark a small circle on each side of the bear where the pack baskets will be glued on. Also mark the back of the pack baskets. Don't paint these areas, as the glue will adhere better on bare wood.

For an added touch, you can carve another larger evergreen, like the one in Santa's pack, for the bear to carry. Hollow the bottom side of it slightly to fit the curve of the bear's pack.

Paint the bear the same way you painted the Adirondack Santa. Use alkyds thinned to a transparent stain with paint thinner.

Paint the muzzle tan with yellow ochre. Use a mixture of burnt umber and black for the bear's coat. Don't make the mixture too dark or opaque. I like the effect of the wood grain showing through slightly to add warmth and depth to the carving. Also, Adirondack black bears always show various shades of brown in their coats.

Use a denser black for the eyes and nose. For a final touch, put a tiny dot of white enamel off to one side of each eye near the top. This suggests a reflection and adds life and sparkle to the eyes.

For the pack baskets use burnt umber. You can add a touch of yellow ochre or raw sienna to make a more golden brown if you like.

Paint the bear's collar red with cadmium red medium.

Use viridian green for the pack strap and the evergreen tree.

If you carved presents in the pack baskets, paint them whatever bright colors appeal to you. Add ribbons with red and gold enamel.

Together, the Adirondack Santa and his bear make a delightful grouping. They always seem to bring a smile to young and old alike.

Swiss St. Niklaus

Several years ago I enjoyed the opportunity of studying woodcarving with the master carvers of Brienz, Switzerland.

This small village is nestled between the mountains and a beautiful glacial lake. Many of the wooden buildings along the cobblestone streets are decorated with ornate carved details—some dating back three hundred years.

As I sat carving at my bench I could gaze out the window and see the shepherds and their flocks high up in the Alpine meadows of the Rothorn Mountain. It was a memorable experience.

What distinguishes the Swiss carving style from any other is the way they carve their small figures, using gouges instead of knives. This is an advanced technique that requires patience, control, and very sharp tools. It leaves the surface of the carving with long flowing cuts that are difficult to achieve with a knife.

This is especially noticeable in facial details, as the eyelids and cheeks have a smooth texture. Each facet left by the tool's edge gently flows into the next. Brienz carvers take great pride in the fineness of their tool marks. They explained to me that sandpaper was only for people who couldn't get their tools sharp.

According to local legends around Brienz, St. Niklaus was an actual person. One account describes him as a holy man living in the mountains, renowned for his wisdom and kindness. Because of his reputation for fairness, he was asked to help unite the feuding cantons of Switzerland, thus ensuring centuries of lasting peace—an achievement for which he is still revered.

In time, his memory blended in folk tradition with tales of the older St. Nicholas of Myra. As a result, Christmas celebrations begin with St. Niklaus Day on December 6. During the night he visits children and leaves gifts of food and small toys. On December 25, the celebrations are very religious, with special church services and family gatherings.

This is a challenging and rewarding project. If you have some carving gouges already, try making St. Niklaus in the Swiss style.

Or, if you like, you can make him with just a knife by carving this pattern the same way as the previous examples.

Either way, it's an opportunity to learn new techniques and have a lot of fun at the same time.

I used air-dried basswood for this project, although you can carve it in white pine. Basswood, or *lindenholz,* as it is called in Switzerland, is the traditional wood for this style of carving.

Many of the cuts necessary to shape the face are made across the grain with a gouge. Basswood is more forgiving and less likely to splinter than pine. Whichever wood you choose, make sure your tools are absolutely razor sharp before you begin.

SWISS ST. NIKLAUS

Tools

Carving knife
10mm no. 14 V-gouge
35mm no. 1 gouge
8mm no. 12 V-gouge
3mm no. 11 veiner
10mm no. 9 gouge
3mm no. 12 V-gouge
6mm no. 9 gouge
1/16-inch drill bit
Pin vise
18mm no. 7 gouge

Materials

Basswood
    6 inches by 2 1/4 inches by 2 inches
Bamboo skewer
    6 inches long, approximately 1/16
        inch in diameter
Semi-gloss spray lacquer
Oil or alkyd paint
    burnt umber
    burnt sienna
    cadmium red medium
    titanium white
    Naples yellow hue
    yellow ochre
    virdian green
Enamel paint
    gold
Acrylic paint
    iridescent gold
    titanium white
    cerulean blue
    burnt umber
    burnt sienna

**Direction
of
wood grain**

**Direction
of
wood grain**

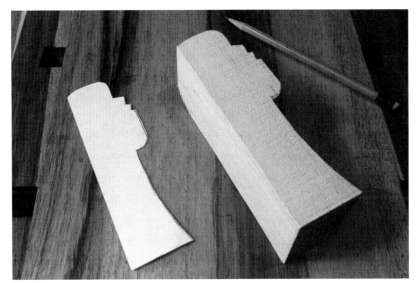

Start with a block of wood 6 inches by 2 ¼ inches by 2 inches. Draw the side view of the pattern on the block and cut it out with a band saw or coping saw. Cutting this view first leaves a flat surface, which makes it easier to saw out the front view later.

To make the second cut, lay the blank down on the flat front surface and trace the outline of the carving on the back. Then place the blank flat on your band-saw table and cut around the lines you have drawn. This produces a blank with a great deal of the waste wood already removed.

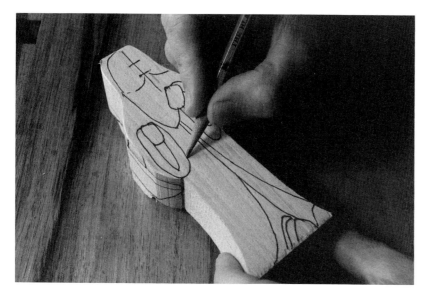

After the blank is cut out, sketch the details of the carving on it. These lines will serve as guides as you begin removing the wood.

Fasten the blank in a vise on your workbench. Then, use a large V-gouge, such as a 10mm no. 14, to outline the sack of gifts St. Niklaus carries.

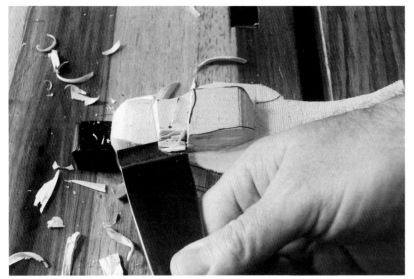

With a large straight gouge, like a 35mm no. 1, rough out the square shapes of the packages. Make vertical cuts about ¼ inch deep along the edges of the packages and the top of the sack. Then use the same tool to pare away the excess wood. Don't worry about being too precise at this point; the packages will be detailed later.

Shape the back of the sleeves with the same tool.

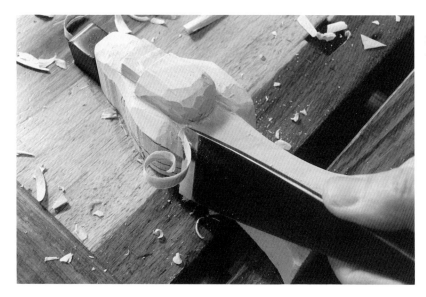

Then, round the back of the robe by taking off the corners with the large flat gouge.

Turn the carving over and fasten it down in the vise again. Begin by outlining the hands and foot with the large V-gouge. Make your cuts about $\frac{1}{8}$ inch deep.

With the large flat gouge, clear away the excess wood, leaving the hands raised. Cut carefully around the hands. You don't want to accidentally chip them off.

Now, outline the sleeves with the V-gouge.

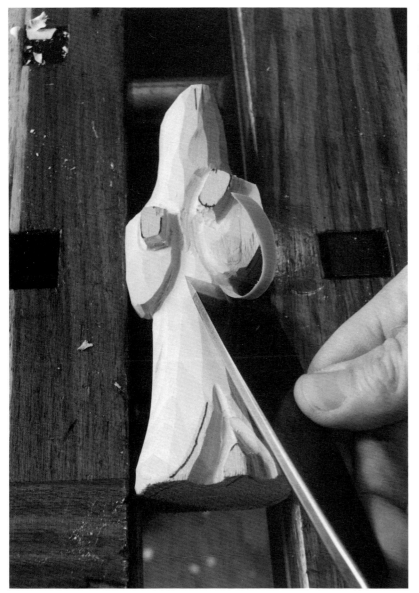

Use the 35mm no. 1 gouge to bevel down the wood around the sleeves, and begin rounding the front of the carving.

Turn the carving sideways in the vise and use the same gouge to round the robe from the side. Notice that I am using the gouge to take one smooth cut from the bottom of the robe right up to the sleeve. These long, flowing cuts are one of the hallmarks of Swiss gouge carving. A master Swiss carver will often shape a figure with cuts that flow the whole length of the carving.

This takes some practice, however, so don't worry if you need to remove the wood in smaller shavings. Being able to handle these large gouges with delicacy and precision is a skill that takes time to develop.

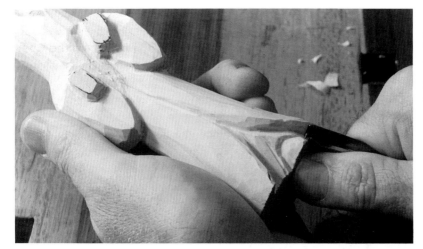

Shape the opening of the robe around the foot with a smaller V-gouge, such as an 8mm no. 12. Use the same tool to shape the foot where it pokes out from under the robes.

To further define the folds of the robe around the foot, I find a U-shaped tool like this 3mm no. 11 veiner helpful. Use it to create the softly rounded folds of the inner robe.

Notice that the thumb of the hand holding the tool is braced on the wood. This gives me a great deal of control. I can take short, very precise cuts with little danger of the tool's slipping. This is an important safety factor, as it provides fine control over the cuts. For more information on the Swiss method of working with gouges, refer to pages 4–5.

The outer robes are folded back in front. To shape the folds, outline them with the 8mm no. 12 V-gouge.

Folds in cloth are not difficult to carve, but it can be hard to picture in your mind exactly how they are formed. Try draping a piece of soft, heavy fabric over something to get a better sense of the shapes.

You can suggest soft folds on the robes by shaping them with an 18mm no. 7 gouge.

Use the same tool to shape flowing folds on the back of the carving. Make these cuts on a slightly curving diagonal rather than straight up and down to suggest the movement of the robes as St. Niklaus walks.

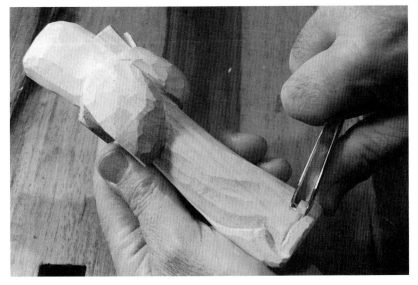

To shape the trim on the bottom edge of the robe, outline it with the 8mm V-gouge. Make this cut quite shallow.

After the bottom part of the figure is shaped, you can move up to the middle section: the sack of gifts, the sleeves, and the hands.

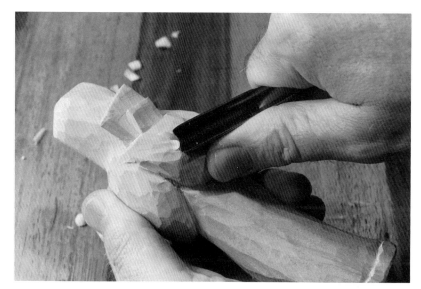

Begin by rounding the sack with a carving knife. Then, make it look soft and bulging by carving diagonal cuts with a curved gouge, such as a 10mm no. 9.

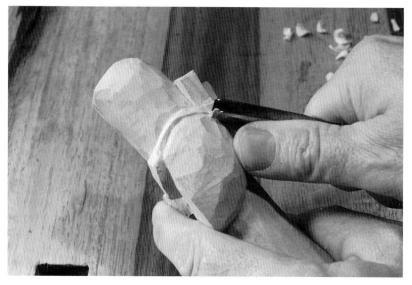

Outline the strap for the sack with the 8mm V-gouge.

Round the shoulder and arm with a knife or flat gouge.

Just smooth off the sharp angles; we will detail the sleeve later.

The technique for carving St. Niklaus's hand is essentially the same as carving the hands of the Adirondack Santa. Review those steps if you're uncertain of the details.

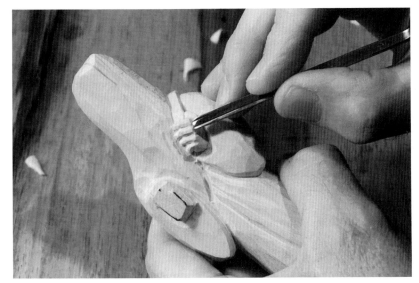

St. Niklaus's left hand is held in a fist holding the strap over his shoulder. Begin by carving the broad planes of the hand with a knife. Then use a 3mm V-gouge to incise three lines to form the fingers.

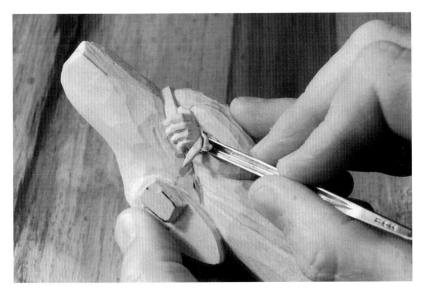

Pencil in a line showing the inner edge of the cuff. Scoop out the wood inside the lines with a small veiner, such as a 3mm no. 11. Because these cuts run right up to the hand, be careful not to scar the finished hand.

Make a stop cut with your carving knife to clean the chips out.

Pencil in the fur trim on the outside of the sleeve. Then, incise a line with the 8mm V-gouge.

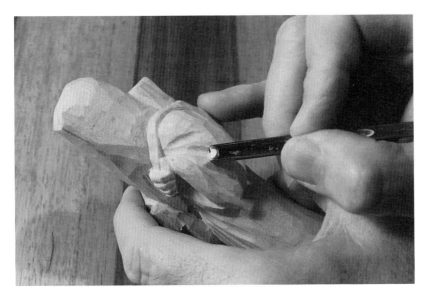

To suggest the arm within the sleeve, carve a few creases with a 6mm no. 9 gouge to show where the elbow bends.

St. Niklaus's right hand holds a staff. Once again, carve the basic shapes of the hand with a knife, and detail the fingers with the small V-gouge.

Then use a small veiner to hollow out the inside of the right sleeve just as you did on the left. Use the 8mm V-gouge to carve the fur trim on the sleeve. Then, add a few creases at the elbow with the 6mm no. 9 gouge.

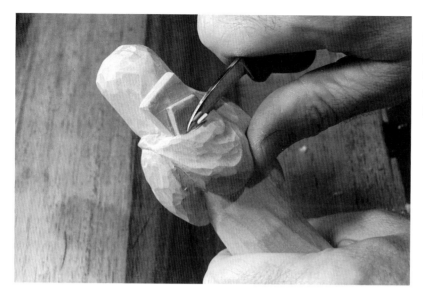

The final step in this section is finishing the packages in the sack. Just use your knife to square up the edges and smooth off any rough spots left by the gouges.

Now you are ready to start the head. The head is turned to the left to give the figure a feeling of movement. Begin by shaping the hood with a knife or flat gouge so that it faces slightly to the left. I find it helpful to draw a centerline on the top of the head angled the way I want the head turned. Then, just carve the hood symmetrically on either side of the line.

Once the head is turned, pencil in some guidelines showing the edge of the hood and indicating the face.

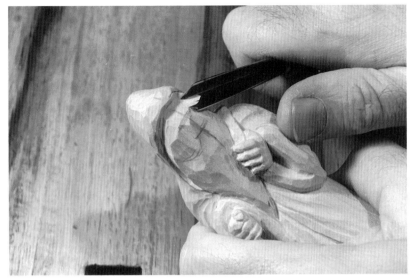

Incise a line along the bottom edge of the hood with the 8-mm V-gouge. By tipping the V-gouge toward the face as you make the cut, you can define the edge of the hood and clear away the excess wood on the face with one cut.

There are two secrets to carving a face in this style: keep your tools razor sharp, and make very delicate cuts.

The first step is to make a long cut on each side of the face with the knife or flat gouge.

Now, the rest of the face will be carved using only the 8mm no. 12 V-gouge. The Swiss carvers who taught me this technique know how to get the maximum usefulness out of each tool.

They never reach for another until they have made every possible cut with the tool already in their hand. Their style inspires me to explore the versatility of each of my own tools to the fullest.

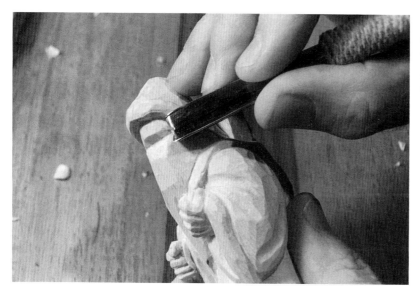

With the V-gouge make one cut about 1/8 inch deep across the bridge of the nose and one cut on either side of it to mark the eye sockets.

Then, make another V cut just under the tip of the nose.

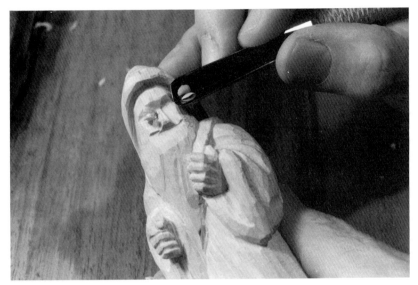

Pencil in lines to mark the two sides of the nose, and incise upward along them with the V-gouge. Then, make a horizontal cut to form the upper eyelid. This cut removes the chips formed when you incised the lines on either side of the nose.

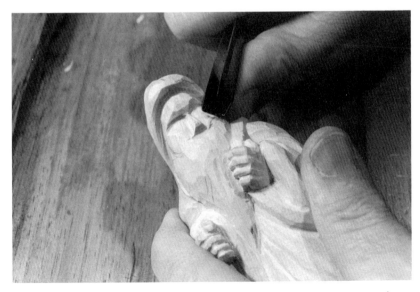

Next, turn the V-gouge on its side and use one edge to flatten the cheeks slightly.

Draw in the outline of the mustache, then outline it with the V-gouge.

Now, pencil in the top edge of the beard, and outline that with the V-gouge.

Once again, use one edge of the V-gouge to smooth the beard and shape the cheeks. Take very tiny shavings when making these cuts and be sure your hands are braced on the wood so that the tool can't slip and take off more wood than you want to.

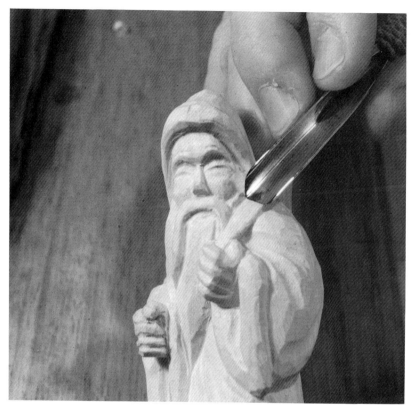

With the same V-gouge, make very tiny, shallow cuts to detail the face. Make one about $\frac{1}{16}$ inch below each upper eyelid to form the bottom lid. Make one just below the mustache to form the bottom lip. Finally, make one above each eye for the eyebrows.

These cuts are exceedingly shallow and delicate. Don't try to measure the depth. The shavings you remove should be paper thin.

After the face is finished, texture the beard and mustache with a small V-gouge, like a 3mm no. 12. Make the cuts long, flowing, and very shallow to suggest a fine, silky beard. You can use the same tool to add small wrinkles to the forehead and beside the eyes.

For a final detail, incise a line around the edge of the hood with the 8mm V-gouge to shape the fur trim.

Make a staff for St. Niklaus out of a sliver of bamboo. Bamboo is stronger than wood in thin sections.

A handy tip for finding thin strips of bamboo is to check your local grocery store for barbecue skewers. Or try a restaurant supply house for the bamboo sticks used to hold fruit in mixed drinks.

To make the staff, cut the bamboo to the proper length, then sand it smooth with fine sandpaper. If you like, you can carve some decorative notches at the top with your carving knife.

Next, very carefully drill a $\frac{1}{16}$-inch hole through the right hand.

I learned a handy method for doing this from the Swiss carvers. Secure the drill bit in a pin vise, a holding device available in hobby shops. Then, hand drill through the wood with a twisting motion of the fingers. Work gently, as too much pressure can split off the hand. This technique gives finer control than using a power drill and puts less pressure on the wood.

Here is a good way to make sure the hole goes down the center of the hand. Partially drill the hole down from the top of the hand—go in just a little way—then partially drill up from the bottom of the hand. Repeat these steps until the two holes meet in the center of the fist.

Then just slip the staff into St. Niklaus's hand.

The painting technique for this St. Niklaus is slightly different from the ones used on the other carvings in this book.

The base coat is alkyds thinned with paint thinner to a transparent stain.

Tint the face and hands with a very dilute mixture of burnt umber and burnt sienna. The paint should just barely color the wood. Then, dry-brush a faint hint of cadmium red medium on the cheeks.

Make the robe a pale, golden-cream color with a mixture of Naples yellow hue and titanium white. Naples yellow hue is like a very soft, light yellow ochre.

Usually I don't mix white with the colors for these oil stains. It tends to make the paint more opaque and covers the wood grain. However, for this carving I want the robe color to hold true over the years as the wood darkens naturally with age. The white paint in this mixture will help ensure that the robe stays light colored.

Paint the lining of the robe where it is folded back the same basic color, darkened slightly with a little more Naples yellow hue.

You can also tone the folds of the robe with this slightly darker golden-cream color. Just brush a little into the folds for added depth.

The trim on the hood, sleeves, and hem of the robe is a golden tan made by darkening Naples yellow hue slightly with yellow ochre.

To create a shadow effect inside the sleeves, mix Naples yellow hue with a little burnt sienna to darken and redden it.

Remember, these colors are all applied as thin washes that just tint the wood. Don't apply the paint in thick layers; it will take forever to dry and make your finished carving look like molded plastic.

The sack on St. Niklaus's back is colored with burnt sienna lightened with a touch of the basic robe color.

The inner robe is a mixture of cadmium red medium and burnt sienna. It should be a rich, deep red. Don't add white to this color or it will look pink.

The boot tip is painted brown with a thin wash of burnt umber. I painted the packages with viridian green and cadmium red

medium. If you like, you can add ribbons with gold enamel. I used Testor's enamel in ¼-ounce jars. It is available at most hobby stores.

Remove the staff from the hand and stain the shaft with burnt umber. Paint the tip gold with enamel.

Allow the alkyd paints to dry overnight. Then, seal the carving with a light application of a spray lacquer, such as Deft Semi-Gloss Wood Finish. For best results, read all the instructions on the can before you begin.

Lightly mist the carving from a distance of about 12 inches. You don't need to create a thick finish on the wood. A very light dusting is enough to seal it.

Sealing the wood is necessary before you add the fine details to the painting because basswood is more porous than pine. If the carving is not sealed, the colors will run with the grain and bleed into each other.

Allow the lacquer to dry for at least thirty minutes.

The fine details will be painted with acrylic paints. Lacquer provides a good base to work on and it seals the wood. I

use acrylics for the details because the texture of the paint is extremely fine. It can be thinned with plenty of water for transparent effects.

I suggest using a magnifier to help you paint these tiny details.

Begin by painting the beard white with titanium white acrylic. Then use an extremely fine 000 sable brush to paint the eyebrows and the whites of the eyes.

For this kind of fine detailing use the best quality brushes you can find. A good quality sable brush holds a fine point and makes painting much easier.

However, if you use your best brushes for acrylics, be sure to keep them moist while you are working and wash them immediately when you finish. Dried acrylic paint ruins a brush.

Give St. Niklaus blue eyes with a tiny dot of cerulean blue.

Enhance the details of your carving with a very transparent mixture of burnt umber and burnt sienna thinned with water. Use a tiny brush to paint fine lines between the fingers to bring out the shapes. It creates a subtle shadow detail.

You can use the same color to darken the lines in St. Niklaus's face slightly. Use a light touch for the most natural effect.

For a final detail, you can add a little sparkle to the carving with a thin wash of iridescent gold acrylic on the robe's trim. Gold acrylic is more subtle and transparent than gold enamel.

When you have completed this project you will have a woodcarving you can display with pride. This is a fairly advanced style of carving. But with a little patience and sharp tools you won't have too much difficulty.

And remember, if this method of carving figures seems tricky at first, don't be discouraged. As I was struggling with my first one, my Swiss teacher kindly patted me on the shoulder and said, "Don't worry, after the first five hundred it gets easier."

Well, I haven't carved five hundred yet, but already it is much easier, and more fun. I really enjoy the challenge of creating a delicate, expressive face with only a few gouges. I think with a little practice, you will, too.

Resources

Albert Constantine & Sons, Inc.
2050 Eastchester Rd.
Bronx, NY 10461
212-792-1600
woodcarving tools and supplies

Brookstone
1655 Bassford Dr.
Mexico, MO 65265-1382
1-800-926-7000
epoxy putty

Christian J. Hummul Co.
P.O. Box 1093
Hunt Valley, MD 21030
1-800-762-0235
alkyd and acrylic paints, brushes, magnifying visors, basswood, knives, woodburning pens, glass eyes, cast feet

Detail Master Burning Systems
2650 Davisson St.
River Grove, IL 60171
708-452-5400
woodburning pens

Garrett Wade
161 Avenue of the Americas
New York, NY 10013
212-807-1155
woodcarving tools and supplies

National Wood Carvers Association
7424 Miami Ave.
Cincinnati, OH 45243
dues include a subscription to Chip Chats, *a bimonthly magazine filled with projects, patterns, and regional news about woodcarving*

P. C. English Enterprises
6201 Mallard Rd. Box 380
Thornburg, VA 22565
703-582-2200
basswood, glass eyes, cast feet, carving supplies

Woodcarvers Supply, Inc.
P.O. Box 7500
Englewood, FL 34295-7500
1-800-284-6229
books, woodburning pens, knives, gouges, sharpening supplies

Woodcraft
  210 Wood County Industrial Park
  P.O. Box 1686
  Parkersburg, WV 26102-1682
  1-800-225-1153
  knives, gouges, sharpening supplies, woodburn-
  ing pens, books, basswood

ABOUT THE AUTHORS

Rick Bütz, who brings some thirty years' carving experience to Stackpole's Woodcarving Step by Step series, recently served as host of the popular PBS series "Woodcarving with Rick Bütz." **Ellen Bütz** is a woodcarver, writer, and photographer; she and Rick have written numerous articles on carving for *Fine Woodworking, Woodworker's Journal, Wood Magazine,* and others. They also are the authors of *How to Carve Wood* and *Woodcarving with Rick Bütz.* They live in a log cabin in the Adirondack Mountains of New York State.